Natural Wonders

By Jan Thurman-Veith
Illustrated by Corbin Hillam

DEDICATION

for Nicholas
with the greatest love
of all

ACKNOWLEDGEMENT:
Special thanks to Bee Huestis and Dave Simon
for their countless hours and treasured friendship

Publisher: Roberta Suid
Editor: Elizabeth Russell
Design and Production: Susan Pinkerton
Cover art: Corbin Hillam

Monday Morning is a registered trademark
of Monday Morning Books, Inc.

ISBN 0-912107-56-1

Printed in the United States of America

9 8 7 6 5 4 3 2 1

Contents

Introduction

Fascination with learning begins almost spontaneously in childhood play. With little effort, parents and teachers can catch the eye and interest of an inquisitive child. However, inborn curiosity must be carefully nurtured and channeled for continued intellectual growth. *Natural Wonders* provides a wealth of ideas and activities for an endless and joyful journey of exploration. The memories of these special experiences can last long after childhood has passed.

Children need to be active and challenged. Unfortunately, today's toy manufacturers too often produce products that invite little or no creative involvement. Children quickly tire of one batch of toys and desire another. This may be good for business, but not for children.

Children need something very different from the kind of passivity taught by mindless toys and television programs. They need activities that urge them to make their own discoveries. They need experiences that build awareness. And most of all, they need time to interact in positive ways with each other.

EXPLORING THE WORLD

Natural Wonders is full of fresh ideas and activities that encourage independent exploration of the world. You will learn how to help young scientists sharpen their observation skills using a variety of inexpensive or free materials. Among the simple-to-do but powerful learning projects are:

- observing spider webs,
- creating color kaleidoscopes,
- building and sailing walnut-shell boats,
- adopting an earthworm, and
- understanding the weather.

The activities in this book animate the simple wonders of everyday life with the magic of imagination. By encouraging creative thinking and play, these hands-on experiences stir the senses, stimulate inquisitiveness, and promote understanding of the world.

The projects are structured to guide wide-eyed children to fun-filled discoveries. Self-esteem and confidence abound as children develop thinking skills through unforced, playful learning.

Along the way, children will gain an awareness of the natural, everyday wonders that we often take for granted. They will build a friendship with nature, a fascination for science, and a lasting love for learning.

5

CREATIVE LEARNING

The activities in this book were designed to encourage the *active* use of imagination in a positive learning environment. These proven activities are more likely to succeed if you keep a few basic ideas in mind.

- Get in touch with the child inside of you and enjoy yourself.
- Maintain a warm and supportive rapport. Close relationships will heighten self-esteem and the spirit of friendship.
- Involve everyone. Shared and cooperative experiences give children a sense of value. Together they discover the joy of accomplishment.
- Grasp moments for teaching. Imaginative play allows each child to begin at his or her own level in the learning process.
- Encourage positive physical contact. It is important for children to touch for development of their sensory-motor systems.
- Believe in the power of imagination. Captivate young children with wide-eyed expressions and a twinkle in your eye.
- Be flexible. Remember, there are no rules. Modify any activity to make it work magically for you and your children.

DISCOVERIES

Animal Affections

Each child chooses an animal to be and then shows the affection the animal might give.

Bear Hug - Wrap arms around someone and give the biggest, strongest, tightest hug bearable.

Butterfly Kiss - Flutter eyelashes on someone's neck.

Caterpillar Squeeze - Wrap someone tightly with whole body and squeeze gently.

Parrot Peck - Give someone a quick, very light kiss on the forehead.

Puppy Love - Hold someone's hand and give a little lick.

Tiger Pat - Roar fiercest roar and pat someone on the back while hugging closely.

"To the man whose senses are alive and alert there is not even the need to stir from one's threshold."

Henry Miller

Believe It Or Not!

It has been said that you will know if someone loves you by pulling the petals from a daisy one by one and saying, "He (or she) loves me," "He loves me not," and so on until the last petal gives you the answer. It can be more fun to let the daisy tell a fortune by asking a question and then pulling the petals as you say, "Yes" and then "No" until the very last petal decides!

Do you believe the magic of daisy fortunes?

Materials: Daisies

"Dreams are the touchstones of our characters."

Henry David Thoreau

Cave Exploration

Imagine that you have been shipwrecked and are now on unfamiliar land, maybe even an unexplored island. As you come up on shore, you see a cave entrance in the side of a mountain. It is dark and cold, but you venture inside, holding hands with your shipmates.

To prepare caves for exploration, simply cut openings in very large cardboard boxes. Connect the boxes with tape, if necessary, and darken the room. You may also add various materials to the cave floors to create a sensation of changing terrain. The explorers may also carry flashlights.

Materials: large cardboard boxes, tape, scissors, materials of various textures, flashlights (optional)

"Originality is unexplored territory. You get there by carrying a canoe. You can't take a taxi."

Alan Alda

11

Choooooooo Choooooooo

This train has an engine, a pull car, a cargo car, many freight cars, some passenger cars, and a caboose. As the children decide what part of the train they will be, line them up and have them connect by holding onto the waist of the person in front of them. Begin very, very slowly. This is a very heavy train. It is fully loaded and must build up its speed and power. *CH CH CH CH CH CH CH CH CH CHCH CHCH CHCH CHCHCHCHCHCHCHCHCHCHCH. Toot! Toot!* The engine leads the train around the track, and the cars follow. On a cold day, let the train run outdoors, and it will become a giant steam engine. *Choooooooo Choooooooo Stop. Back up. Go again. Head for a tunnel. Duck!*

Echo echo echo echo

Separate the children into rooms or places where they cannot see each other. In unison, one group calls out to another. When the next group hears, it calls out, and farther away another group hears and calls out until the echo finally fades away into the distance. Try to place children where they can barely hear the echo so the sound will have to travel a distance between them.

If using only one child at each location, let each one have a tube to call through. It's best to think of short, concise phrases to begin.

Materials: cardboard tubes (optional)

"The events of childhood do not pass, but repeat themselves like seasons of the year."

Eleanor Farjeon

Feely Stories

Let the children help prepare bowls of various foods. It is best to choose foods with interesting textures. For example:

grapes
lettuce leaves
dry cereal flakes
tomato wedges
peeled banana slices
noodles
Jello
hard boiled eggs
whole coconut

Turn down the lights and tell a "Feely Story." The story below is supposed to be scary but fun. Think up other original stories. Pass the bowls around in the darkened room, and let the children touch as their imaginations run wild.

Once upon a time in a pretend place far, far away was a girl (or boy) who went for a long, long walk. She came to an old haunted house. No one lived there. It was a very tall house with open shutter windows and squeaky doors.

She went in. She couldn't see. It was dark. She went up some stairs and down some stairs and around some stair corners. Then she stopped. She opened the door and reached in. She felt some hair (noodles). She quickly closed the door and ran up some stairs and down some stairs and around some stair corners. Then she stopped.

She opened the door and reached in. She felt some eyes (grapes). She quickly closed the door and ran up some stairs and down some stairs and around some stair corners. Then she stopped. She opened the door and reached in. She felt a face (coconut). Continue as long as you like with the story.

FINALLY, she went up some stairs and down some stairs and around some stair corners. Then she stopped. She opened the door and reached in. She didn't feel anything. She didn't hear anything. Then something touched her on the shoulder and said, "Tag, you're it!" Reach out and touch someone when you say "Tag, you're it!"

*This story is especially good for young children because it has repetition, anticipation, and a surprise but harmless ending. Adding the tactile sense gives the story another level of interest.

Materials: various foods, bowls

"When someone demands blind obedience, you'd be a fool not to peek."

Jim Fiebig

A Foot Long

Measure 12 inches and then let the children cut out the shape of a foot or shoe. They may want to decorate it as a ballet slipper, a hiking boot, or a tennis shoe — but it is one foot, nevertheless! Now they can take their one foot measurement and explore their world to find things that are a foot long. *What do you think might be two feet long? Let's measure. How about five feet? How long is your arm? How long is your body? How tall is your Dad? How big is your car?*

Materials: ruler, paper, crayons, scissors

"The essential thing is not to find, but to absorb what we find."

Paul Valery

A Frame-Up

Show the children how to make a frame by touching their fingers and thumbs together from both hands and looking through. With these frames they can capture pictures worth a thousand words! Go for a walk framing flowers, leaves, tree bark . . . and don't forget to frame a beautiful picture of the ground and the creatures that are hiding there. Now lie on your back on an early spring day or a stormy winter afternoon and then watch the clouds on parade. Each one is a unique float that you can capture in your own frame of nature.

"I walk in the garden, I look at the flowers and shrubs and trees and discover in them an exquisiteness of contour, a vitality of edge or a vigor of spring as well as an infinite variety of color that no artifact I have seen in the last sixty years can rival . . . each day as I look, I wonder where my eyes were yesterday."

Bernard Berenson

Goin' Fishin'

Use a dowel for a fishing pole and attach a string with a magnet tied to the end as a hook. Attach paper clips to paper fish. Be sure to put the imaginary worm on the hook before tossing the line into the water! Now wait patiently until there is a bite. *Whoa, it's a big one. Don't let it get away. What kind is it?*
*The educational value of this activity may be expanded by using fish of different colors or adding numbers, shapes, or pictures.

Imaginary fishing is fun, too. One child pretends to fish while the others swim around in the pond. When a child is touched with the hook (magnet), he or she is caught and must roll out of the pond and onto the shore.

As a science project, have the children experiment with paper, pennies, sponges, paper clips, scissors, etc. to see what is attracted to the magnet. Then the children can go "fishing" to find metal objects around the room.

I can fish
Right here in this lake.
I have worms and a pole,
That's all that it takes.

I wait and I watch
'Til I get a bite
Then reel a big one in
With all my might.

Materials: dowels, string, magnets with holes in the center, paper fish, paper clips

"Too often we give children answers to remember rather than problems to solve."

Roger Lewin

19

Many Friendly Dragons

This is an activity for a cold, frosty winter day. Create scaly dragon bodies out of egg cartons strung together and tied around the children's necks with yarn. Add egg carton ears or horns by stringing individual egg holders with yarn and then attaching them like a hat. Paint everything green or purple or a favorite dragon color. Bundle up and race out the door, blowing big puffs of steamy dragon breath all the way.

Materials: egg cartons, scissors, paint, yarn

"Any adult who spends even fifteen minutes with a child outdoors finds himself drawn back to his own childhood, like Alice falling down the rabbit hole."

Sharon MacLatchie

Mini-Maps

Let the children press their thumbs onto an ink pad and then onto a piece of white paper. The fascinating "mini-map" can be a source of intrigue for an imaginary tiny traveler. Who are these travelers? Where are they going? What big, big things do they see on their wee journey?

The children may add tiny faces, ears, tails, feet, wings, scales, etc. to their thumbprints to create many mini-creatures. Imagine the life of a teensy tiny thumbprint mouse! Would he swim in a teaspoon? Would he sleep in a thimble?

Materials: ink pad, white paper

"Originality exists in every individual because each of us differs from the others...

Jean Guitton

Musical Monsoon

Use instruments and add kitchen utensils to create a musical monsoon. Begin with the sounds of a gentle breeze and soft rain. Slowly build up to howling winds, crashing thunder, and a torrential downpour. Let the storm die away to light showers. Look for the rainbow!

Darken the room to help the children enjoy the full sound sensations of their musical monsoon.

Materials: inventive instruments, pots, pans, lids, spoons, etc.

"In music one must think with the heart and feel with the brain."
George Szell

Painting the World

Give each child a cup of water and a brush. The children decide what color of imaginary paint to use and may change colors as often as they like. Have them start by painting the fence or the sidewalk. They will become very busy and will soon have everything painted brightly in imaginary colors. Help them "see" the colors in their minds by having them tell what colors they used and what pictures they painted.

I'll paint the world
For all to see;
Bright and bold
The colors will be.
Here is my bucket,
A brush and a place
To make magical pictures
That won't leave a trace.

Materials: cups of water, brushes

"Every child is an artist. The problem is how to remain an artist once he grows up."

Pablo Picasso

Pop! Pop! Popcorn!

Create a "popper" by marking a circle on the floor with tape or a hoop. Put a few children inside the circle as "kernels," fresh and cool in the bottom of the popper, with their bodies curled up tight. Pour a few tablespoons of imaginary oil over them. The other children sit around the popper, wiggling their fingers to make the fire and saying "sssss" to make the oil sizzle. Then wait and listen, as the kernels get hotter and hotter and finally . . . POP! One child bursts up and flies out of the popper, and then the next and the next until the kernels have all popped out of the popper. Eat the "air popcorn." Mmmmm - tasty and fun!

Materials: tape or hoop for imaginary popper

Put a sheet in the middle of the floor with a popcorn popper in the center. Have the children sit around the edge of the sheet, well away from the popper. As the kernels start to pop, remove the lid, and let the popcorn fly! The popper will be hot. Have the children stay seated, and the popcorn will come within their reach. Flying popcorn — yum yum!

> Pop, pop, popcorn,
> Are you getting hot?
> Sizzle, sizzle
> Wiggle, wiggle . . .
> Fly out of the pot!

Materials: sheet, popcorn popper, popcorn

"Fly pleasures and they will follow you."
Benjamin Franklin

Rock Walk

Set out to find rocks. Each child will find his own that is special to him. Although rocks do not appear to be alive, they are a very important part of the cycle of change. The children may share their rocks and look for the differences in shape, color, size, texture, and personalities! Pet your rock and find the comforting feelings of touch. Put it in your pocket and rub it often. It feels good! Put all of the rocks in one small area and let each child find his own rock by touching only.

Materials: rocks

"What nobody sees is rarely found."

Pestalozzi

Scavenger Hunt

Send everyone out to find pebbles, seed pods, a handful of sand, twigs, rocks, pine needles, leaves, pine cones (etc.) and also anything left by those dreadful "litterbugs." When each child has a collection, display the findings on the floor or a large table top. Then, individually or in a group, make a mosaic. First draw a simple pattern (a butterfly or rooster, for example) on a piece of cardboard with a felt marker. Then glue on the materials to form different colors, textures, and parts of the mosaic until the entire area is covered. Stand back and admire this rare art form. *Well done!*

Materials: cardboard cut in pieces, glue, bags for collecting materials, felt marker

"The best measure of success is not an expensive car or high-price clothes, but how your children describe you to their friends."

Bob Batz

Scientific Explanations

Young children are very aware of the many natural events that surround them. However, their explanations of how these occur may be somewhat less than scientific. Some children have well-thought-out answers, while others consider the phenomenon and without a moment's hesitation give you a response that is perfectly logical — in the mind of a child.

Consider these: thunder, lightning, fog, wind, clouds, magnetism, gravity, rain, stars, moon.

Stars (by Diane, age 3) Peepholes for Santa. He watch you sleep.

Lightning (by Alaina, age 4) I don't know but it can scare your ears off!

Rain (by Michelle, age 4) God gets mad and makes all the angels cry.

Gravity (by Eric, age 4) Oh, I remember. What makes us not float away? Food, that's it. Food, we eat it and then stay down.

Rain (by Stephen, age 4) It just comes down for no reason. Somebody poked a hole and it falls right on top of us. I better ask my mom.

Materials: paper, pen to record responses

Treasure Hunt

Tell the children a story of a hidden treasure that can only be found by following clues. Make a picture card (clue) to lead them to the first landmark. For example:

Each landmark has a clue that directs them to the next. After many clues, the hunters will finally find the "treasure" (such delights as balloons, stickers, etc.). It's actually the adventure they love more than the treasure!

Materials: paper, crayons, treasures

"What we want is to see the child in pursuit of knowledge, and knowledge in pursuit of the child."

George Bernard Shaw

Turtle Tales

Have each child choose an animal that will be part of a story. With a paring knife, cut potato stamps for the parts of the body for each animal. By using separated body parts, children can make the animals in different positions and poses. After telling the story, have children press the various parts of their animals onto an ink pad, then onto storybook pages. Print the story along the bottom of the pages.

*To help the children get started on a story, present them with a problem situation, such as a talking teddy bear who had just moved into a new neighborhood in the forest, or a forgetful frog who couldn't find his way home to the pond, or a bunny rabbit who couldn't think of a gift for her mother. The main character of the story may meet each of the other animal characters along the way.

Materials: potatoes, paring knife, ink pad, storybook paper

"Imagination is the eye of the soul."

Joseph Joubert

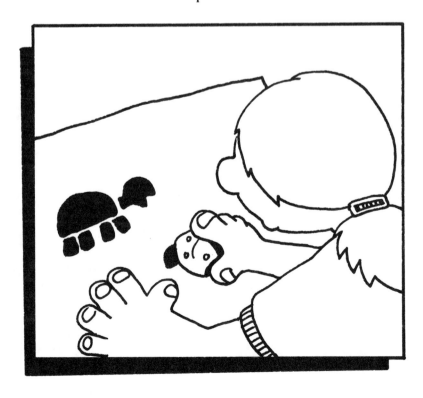

Wanted

Put up a "Wanted" poster and send your "detectives" out to find the person described in the poster. The children will have to think carefully about the description to be sure that they find the right "suspect."

Materials: paper, crayons

"People have one thing in common: they are all different."

Robert Zend

Web Watchers

Take a field trip outside to watch the birds, bugs, and spider, or just each other! Binoculars help the children focus on the details of the world. Have them lie face down to watch a tiny bug crawl slowly up a blade of grass or a spider spin a web.

To make binoculars for better viewing, paint two toilet paper rolls with bright colors. When dry, tape them together at both ends and punch holes on the outsides to attach a yarn strap.

Materials: toilet paper rolls, paint, tape, hole punch, yarn

"I'm always ready to learn although I do not always like being taught."

Sir Winston Churchill

Wild Pet Show

Have each child bring a pet that is found in the "wild" in nature. The children should provide safe, natural settings for their pets while in captivity. Pets are proudly displayed by the children and then judged on categories such as most wiggly, slimiest, longest legs, fastest crawler, ugliest, prettiest, biggest, smallest, most unusual — and any other categories desired. The winning owners receive ribbons, and, of course, everyone wins! Have the children return the pets to their natural homes at the end of the day.

Materials: paper ribbons, wild pets, extra jars, caps for food and water

"A three-year-old child is a being who gets almost as much fun out of a fifty-six dollar set of swings as it does out of finding a small green worm."

Bill Vaughan

Wilderness Expeditions

With the help of fellow wilderness adventurers, have everyone scale an imaginary cliff (a fence, wall, or other obstacle) by boosting, pushing, holding and pulling each other up and over. Let the children find their own ways to accomplish this feat. (Stand by as an observer for safety only.)

Have the children try crossing a log (a board or strip of tape on the floor) over an imaginary rushing river. They must balance and hold each other tightly as they traverse this treacherous natural bridge to the cliff and back again.

Materials: obstacles for cliff, log

"I know of no more encouraging fact than the unquestionable ability of man to elevate his life by a conscious endeavor."

Henry David Thoreau

EXPERIMENTS

Adopt a Tree

A local nursery will often donate a small tree for a group of children to plant. Provide shovels to break the hard ground or soak the area with water. Have the children dig with their own hands. Together they can set the tree in its new home. Cover it with dirt and give it water. Watching the tree change will provide an understanding of seasons and weather. The children may gain a sense of the struggles, hardships, and new growth a tree experiences, also. Visit the tree often and bring it water. Talk to the tree. Slip into its limbs for a big hug! Most children call it "My Tree" and years later will return with fond memories of its adoption.

Materials: tree, shovels

"There are only two lasting bequests we can hope to give our children. One of these is roots; the other, wings."
Hodding Carter

Animal Trackers

Have the children use their hands and feet to make animal paw, hoof, or foot prints with paint on strips of paper. Let them experiment with different body parts that will make an impression of the tracks of some wild and not-so-wild beasts. Then have some of the children lay a trail of prints for the other animal trackers to follow.

Materials: paint, paper

"Art flourishes where there is a sense of adventure."

Alfred North Whitehead

Bubble Bursting

Prepare the bubble solution below. Use the wands found in purchased bubbles, and then experiment with other objects for different and unusual effects. Instead of blowing the bubbles, try waving the object through the air and watch the bubbles being released.

Bubble Solution: Put about one inch of clean water in a shallow tub. Gently mix in five or six squirts of dishwashing detergent. Stir in some sugar until it is dissolved to increase the surface tension of the soapy water. Gather around and enjoy!

*After bubble play, it is fun to become giant bubbles. Any opening can serve as the life-size bubble machine (a cylinder, a hula hoop, or even a closet). The bubble machine blows out huge bubbles in the shape of children that float and bounce and then land lightly on the floor . . . and then burst! *All gone. Disappeared!!!* Make double bubbles the next time and have all of the bubbles join together in a multiple bubble, then burst one by one or all at once.

"Childhood is the sleep of reason."

Rousseau

Butterfly Garden

Plant a special garden that will attract butterflies of many kinds. The beautiful butterflies will share your garden area to collect nectar for food. Ask your local nursery which plants will grow best in your area and climate. Here are a few possibilities:

Flowering Plants
mints
zinnias
marigolds
true asters
sunflowers
Peruvian verbena
lippia
petunias
alyssum
sweet William
primrose

Woody Plants
buddleia
coyote bush
escallonia
lilac
milkweeds
hollyhock

Wild Plants
vetch
stock
wild mustard
lupines
wild sweet pea

Thanks to the University of California, Davis for this list.

Materials: garden tools, flower seeds, rain, sunshine

Color Creations

Give the children samples of the basic colors: red, yellow, blue, and white. In separate containers, let them mix colors to try and find the combinations to make green, grey, pink, purple, and orange.

How do you make a bright color into a pastel? (add white) What three colors might make tan or peach? (red, white, and yellow) What color works best to darken colors? (purple) What colors make something yucky when you mix them together?

*Having the children experiment with color mixing instead of telling them which colors work gives them the fascination of discovery, which will be remembered long after the activity is over.

Materials: small containers, mixing sticks, paints

"Great lessons are learned usually in simple and everyday ways."

Pearl S. Buck

A Day at the Snail Races

Have each child bring a snail found in the yard or neighborhood to enter in the big race. A smooth tabletop makes a good track. Set the finish line about three feet from the start. Put little snail nibbles (fresh leaves) beyond the finish line to encourage the snails to go the length of the track. Mark the snails on their shells.

Let the race begin. *On your mark, get set, go! Go! Go! Oh well, we might want to check back later to see how the race is going...* All owners are awarded participation ribbons, and all snails must go back to their homes when the race is over.

Materials: snails, leaves, paint or colored stickers, ribbons

"By perseverance the snail reached the ark."

Charles Haddon Spurgeon

For Better and For Worse

Grow pairs of plants from seeds in small pots. It's important for each child to have his or her own to watch during this experiment. Give the plants everything they need to thrive: good soil, sunlight, water, and attention. Watch the plants as the first bit of life breaks through the soil and reaches up toward the sunshine. This has been "for better." Then see what happens when you continue to give care to one plant but neglect the other by depriving it of sunlight or water. *What happens? How can you tell what the plant is missing? What if you give it too much sunlight or water? What happens? How can you tell what has happened by looking at the plant? Did it get dry and crackly, or did it droop? Did it change color or shrivel up or burn on the edges? How long did it take? Which plant was for better and which one for worse? All living things need tender loving care to live a long, healthy life. What do you need and who takes care of you?*

Materials: pots, seeds, soil

"Nature is visible thought."

Heraclitus

Rain Dance

Many years ago when the Indians needed rain for their corn and crops, they would do a rain dance. They believed if they danced and chanted to the gods of nature, rain would pour down from the skies. But we know today that rain falls when warm air rises and hits cold air. Small drops of water form, and when they get too heavy, they fall to the ground.

Show how clouds form in the sky by making a little cloud in a jar. Put about one inch of hot water in a large jar and put a metal pan of ice cubes on top. Then place the jar carefully in a dark place and use a flashlight to look for the cloud. Keep watching to see the tiny raindrops gather and fall to the bottom. Do a rain dance and enjoy the gift from the nature gods!

Materials: large jar with wide mouth, flashlight, water, pan of ice cubes

"Education is the instruction of the intellect in the laws of Nature."

Thomas Henry Huxley

The Royal Garden

Arrange small pieces of charcoal, broken brick, porous rock, or cellulose sponge over the bottom of a glass pie tin. Mix together ½ cup water, ½ cup salt, ½ cup liquid bluing, and 1 cup ammonia. Use caution and never sniff the ammonia! Pour the magical garden mixture very carefully over the base material until it is moistened. Then squeeze a few drops of blue, green, and yellow food coloring on top of the charcoal to bring the colors of spring to the royal garden. In a few days it will "bloom" with gems for a king or queen!

*If possible, view your garden daily with a magnifying glass.

Materials: glass pie tin, pieces of charcoal, water, salt, bluing, ammonia, food coloring (not red)

"A mother understands what a child does not say."

Jewish proverb

Shadow Partners

On a bright, sunny day, take the children outside and pair them up with "shadow partners." Taking turns, each partner traces the other's shadow on the sidewalk with chalk. After an hour or so, have them trace each other's shadow again. What happened? Did the shadow partner grow taller? Shorter? In the late afternoon, shadows become giants with long, long legs! Make the giant move and turn and swing his arms.

Materials: chalk

"The art of teaching is the art of assisting discovery."

Mark Van Doren

Sock Express

Collecting seeds on socks is an enjoyable way to learn how seeds travel. Have each child bring in an old pair of wool socks. Put the socks on over the shoes and go for a walk outside, through a field or along a weedy area. The socks will collect seeds, burrs, stickers, and weeds of all kinds. Take the socks off and carefully pull off all of the "hitchhikers." See what came along for the ride!

Materials: wool socks

"Few things are commonplace in themselves. It's our reaction to them that grows dull."

Arthur Gordon

Solar Baking

Solar baking is not a quick process, but the naturally dried foods are delicious. You may want to try apples to begin, but bananas, peaches, apricots, and grapes may also be baked in the sun.

First, peel and core several apples, at least one for each person. Then slice the apples thinly crosswise to make rings. Next, place the apple rings on a clean cloth outdoors on a table in direct sunlight. Use a cheesecloth cover to protect the fruit from insects. Allow the fruit to dry until dusk, then bring it indoors if the night will bring moisture. Return the fruit to the sun the next day and continue drying, this time on the other side. If you live in a hot area, the apple slices should be ready in a few days. Enjoy them as a natural treat, Mother Nature's candy!

Materials: fresh fruits, knife, cloth for drying, cheesecloth

"We cannot fail in following nature."

Montaigne

Trails of Timber

Send out a group of trailblazers to make a trail for the others to follow. The trailblazers will need to gather sticks, branches, rocks, and other natural things to use as signs of the trail.

For example, a pile of rocks with a feather sticking out of the top could mean "water ahead" (pond or fountain). Sticks forming arrows could be used to point out the direction of the trail. After the children have laid their trail signs, let them track each other on nature trails through the backyard or a nearby park.

Materials: natural trail markers

"The object of education is to prepare the young to educate themselves throughout their lives."

Robert Maynard Hutchins

Unsinkable Molly Brown

For this experiment, put a cloth in the bottom of a large glass. You can draw a picture of "Molly" on the cloth if you like. Turn the glass upside down and push it straight down in water. You can use a tub or pool filled with water, or even a big pot. *What has happened to Molly Brown? Is she wet?* Lift the glass from the water and check the cloth. How did it stay dry? Was Molly Brown unsinkable? (The water does not get in because the air inside the glass takes up all of the space!)

Next, draw a boat on the cloth. Repeat the same steps, but allow the glass to tilt. *Uh oh. Here it is, the ship Titanic going down. What happened?*

Materials: large glass, cloth, container of water

"The only way to discover the limits of the possible is to go beyond them to the impossible."

Arthur C. Clarke

GAMES

Body Bridges

Help the children construct human bridges, using each other as their only building blocks. Arms, legs, or whole bodies can be used to form the arch and the necessary supports. See how many different bridges can be built by the Body Bridges Engineering Company. Sometimes a weary bridge will collapse, so watch out for bridges built over water. *Was that London Bridge falling down? Are there any sharks below? What other bridges can you build?*

"One of the greatests sources of energy is pride in what you are doing."

Spokes

Body Weaving

Have all but one of the children connect by holding hands. Any position is okay — standing or sitting, bending or lying down — as long as the connection holds. The remaining child is the weaver who goes between the bodies, in and out, in and out, until he or she reaches the end and then returns the same way. The weaver may have to go over arms and under legs or over legs and under arms. Take turns weaving. A ribbon or string can be used to see the pattern as it is woven.

Materials: ribbon or string (optional)

"No one knows what he can do till he tries."

Publilius Syrus

A Butterfly is Born

Wrap one child loosely in a sheet. Then tell the familiar story of the caterpillar in its dark, warm cocoon. Describe how the long body changes. As its wings grow, its antennae begin to sense the world around it, and its eyes open slowly. Finally, the caterpillar emerges from the cocoon a beautiful butterfly, as you pull the edge of the sheet, letting the child roll free. Fly away, fly away, butterfly!

Materials: sheet

"We couldn't conceive of a miracle if none had ever happened."

Libbie Fudim

Caterpillar-Hug Walk

Children sit in a line with their legs wrapped around the person in front of them. All parts ready? Give a big squeeze. Now try to walk by lifting each side of your bottom up and forward. This takes some teamwork for everyone to move together. Try starting with pairs of children. Once they learn how to do it, add on to the caterpillar.

"Go ahead and do the impossible. It's worth the look on the faces of those who said you couldn't."

Walter Bagehot

Copycats

Everyone "copycats" the actions and sounds of the leader. The leader sings the rhyme below. Go first to give the children examples of the range of sounds and movements possible. Use any sounds that are fun to make and within the children's ability to imitate. The motions should involve body parts moved in different ways. Repeat the same sounds and movements until everyone is able to imitate. Repeat the musical rhyme and begin again.

*This is a wonderful activity for even the introverted child because the copycats imitate anything and everything — bashful arm-folding and shy smiles, as well as intentional movements and sounds. Success is guaranteed!

Copycat, Copycat
That's what I am.
Copycat, Copycat
Do what _____ does, if you can!
            (child's name)

"Leadership is action, not position."

David D. McGannon

57

Human Beans

A few children pretend that they are seeds buried under the warm, moist soil in the garden. They are quiet and sleeping, curled up tightly, eyes closed in the darkness. The sun (another child) comes out and calls to the little seeds, "Wake up, wake up, little seeds." The seeds start to open very slowly . . . but then fall back to sleep. Other children pretend to be clouds. They see that the little seeds are still not awake. The clouds gently sprinkle raindrops on the little seeds, which begin to stretch and finally stand up. The sun comes back, and the little seeds reach up and out, growing roots and leaves until they are big and strong. And finally we can see what kind of seeds they are! Did the seeds grow into flowers or trees or vegetables? What kinds?

*As you direct the children through the growing experience, consider using sound and lighting for further sensory stimulation. Make the room dark when the seeds are underground, and then turn on the lights when the sun comes out. Use tingling or light tapping sounds for the sprinkling rain.

Human beans
Under the ground,
Quiet and dark,
Not a sound.

Here comes the rain,
And now the sun.
Wake up little ones;
Your time has come.

Grow strong and tall;
Dig roots deep, send branches high.
Open your leaves,
And look up to the sky.

Wake up! Wake up!

"Never does nature say one thing and wisdom another."

Juvenal

Human Magnets

Have the children become "human magnets." One child is the magnet and moves through the room. The magnet attaches to the other children until the whole group is clustered together.

"That person proves his worth who can make us want to listen when he is with us and think when he is gone."

Grit

Kid Connections

Each child finds a partner. As you call out body parts, each child connects with his or her partner: "Toe to toe! Elbow to elbow! Knee to knee!" Then try calling "finger to shoulder" or "lips to ear" or "heel to back." Experiment with connecting cheeks, thighs, and knuckles.

*The children will watch and learn as they successfully bond in these "kid connections." They will discover more and more body parts and all the ways these different parts move, bend, twist, turn.

"To be able to be caught up into the world of thought — that is to be educated."

Edith Hamilton

Lost in Space

Darken the room for this outer space experience. The children begin in a group on the floor. Help them imagine how it would feel to float, weightless and free, in outer space. The children will begin turning and rolling in all different directions. As the darkness closes in, the children must find each other, hold hands, and collect again in a group. No sounds are allowed. Together they return to the light and gravity of Earth.

"When it is dark enough, you can see the stars."

Ralph Waldo Emerson

Mirror, Mirror

Standing face to face, the children imitate each other's movements. Have them take turns being the reflection and the person looking into the mirror. They should move slowly and keep a close eye on their mirror images while making identical whole-body movements and facial expressions.

"You can observe a lot just by watching."

Yogi Berra

Punching Pal

Fill an old pillow case with newspaper or soft cloth and tie the end closed with a piece of rope. Leave enough rope to hang the bag from the bar on a swing set or any place that will be spacious enough for the bag to swing. Here is a punching bag for junior boxers. Make boxing gloves from lunch bags. Pad the bags with newspaper and tie securely around the child's wrists. This is often a favorite activity for a child who is angry and needs to let out some feelings or frustrations.

Materials: pillow case, newspaper or soft rags, thin rope; lunch bags, yarn or string

"I start where the last man left off."

Thomas Edison

Row Your Boat

Each child finds a partner. Have the pair sit face to face and toe to toe, holding hands. As one person leans back, the other leans forward. Keep up this rowing motion while singing "Row, Row, Row Your Boat." Then begin an adventure across the lake or down the river. *Watch out for the rapids! Whoa, we're tipping over. Splash! Swim to shore!*

"Is life not a hundred times too short for us to bore ourselves?"
Friedrich Nietzsche

Talking Chalkboard

Each child finds a partner. Once child becomes a "talking chalkboard" by sitting with his back to the other child and leaning forward (or lying face down). The "writer" puts shapes, numbers, or letters on the chalkboard (the child's back) using an index finger as chalk. The talking chalkboard identifies the written symbols.

*If children have difficulty identifying the symbol traced on their backs, put examples on cards in front of them as a visual aid. Limit the choices to two or three, and choose symbols or shapes that are dissimilar to make discrimination easier.

Materials: cards with letters, shapes, numbers, or symbols

"A man with a new idea is a crank, until the idea succeeds."

Mark Twain

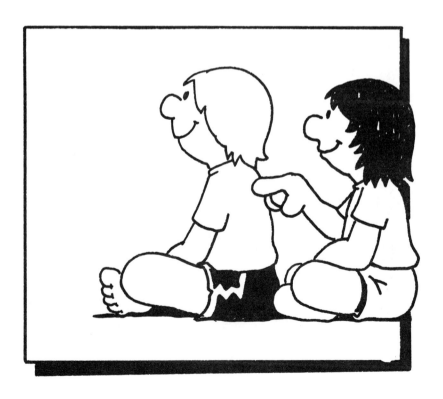

Toss and Catch

Cut bleach bottles into scoops. Use a tennis ball and the scoops to play a game of toss and catch. This is an inexpensive way to give children a challenging game that develops their eye-hand coordination and motor development. It is also important for children to see how throw-away items may be recycled into imaginative toys.

Materials: bleach bottles, knife, tennis balls

"The man is richest whose pleasures are the cheapest."

Henry David Thoreau

Tune-up Shop

Bring your body in for a tune-up. Tell the mechanics what part(s) aren't working — the part you kick with, the part you smell with, your wheels (feet), or shocks (legs). The crew will find the part and repair it (with mechanical massage) and you'll soon be on the road again!

"He who has imagination without learning has wings and no feet."

Joseph Joubert

Tying the Knot

The children hold hands and form a circle. One child begins by going over or under locked hands. Another child does the same, pulling the rest of the group along. The children keep crossing over, under, around, and through until there are no more openings, and the circle has become one big, tangled knot. Hang on tight and begin to untie the knot without breaking hands.

*To incorporate communication and spatial relations skills, ask one child to watch as the knot is tied and then give specific directions to get everyone out of the tangled mess.

"Whether you believe you can do a thing or not, you are right."
Henry Ford

Wheelbarrows

The children find partners. One child of each pair is the wheelbarrow, and the other is the farmer who pushes the wheelbarrow to the garden. The wheelbarrow is on his hands and knees with palms on the floor. The farmer lifts up the wheelbarrow by the handles (ankles) and together they begin to move slowly forward.

*This activity may be too difficult for younger children who have not yet developed the arm and shoulder strength required. If so, you can be the wheelbarrow and let many farmers push you along! The children will have a chance to be wheelbarrows when they grow bigger and stronger. This is a wonderful cooperative experience for brothers and sisters to try, too.

"Success is a journey, not a destination."

Ben Sweetland

70

INVENTIONS

Architects and Carpenters

Have the children design and build a model building or city. Ask everyone to bring in cardboard boxes, wood scraps, straws, spools, and other similar leftovers. These can be used to form buildings, sidewalks, smokestacks, stairways, windows . . . who knows? Bring in cans of sand or boxes of dirt for "fields" and encourage the children to add trees, fences, and animals. Supply a few small cars and trucks, and the children may design roads and bridges.

*Let the architects and carpenters become completely involved in their materials. This is a creative project that gives every child a feeling of accomplishment and success while discovering relationships among objects, balance, and dimensions.

Materials: boxes, wood scraps, straws, spools, empty cans, meat trays, cartons, cups, etc. for construction materials; white glue and clay for cement, dirt and sand, small cars, animals, or people (optional)

"Production is not the application of tools to materials, but logic to work."

Peter Drucker

Color Kaleidoscopes

Cut two pieces of waxed paper in equal circles about five inches in diameter. Scrape shavings from brightly colored crayons, and sprinkle onto one piece of the waxed paper. Cover with the other piece and press in between sheets of newspaper. Use a dry, warm iron. Lift and check to see that the colors are melted. If necessary, press again. Wrap the waxed paper over the end of a toilet paper roll, and secure with a rubber band or tape. Trim the excess paper, if desired. Take the kaleidoscope to a light source and peer through. Look into each other's kaleidoscopes to see the different patterns and colors.

Materials: waxed paper, iron, crayons, scissors, rubber bands or tape, toilet paper rolls

"The real voyage of discovery consists not in seeing new lands, but in seeing with new eyes."

Marcel Proust

The Fix-It Shop

Find something broken — an old appliance, a chair, or a vehicle (wagon, tricycle, bike, etc.). Let the children fix it with pliers, screwdrivers and masking tape. Let each child work on a different broken item. When they're finished, they'll charge you for "parts and labor," so be ready to pay plenty.

Materials: "broken" items, tools (pliers, screwdrivers, etc.), tape

"Though pride is not a virtue, it is the parent of many virtues."

M.C. Collins

Incredible Edibles

A creative and tasty incredible edible is as much fun to build as it is to eat!

Tinker Toy Towers: Straight pretzel sticks and chunks of cheese are the only building materials needed.

Peanut Butter Playdough: Mix together 1 cup peanut butter, ⅔ cup honey, and ½ cup instant non-fat dry milk. Use hands to form, roll, and shape. Cover the table surface with waxed paper (taped down) for easy clean-up. Mmmmm, good!

Muffin Faces: On an English muffin, create a face with a variety of ingredients — cheese slices, olives, tomato wedges, pizza sauce, anchovies, pepperoni — then toast in a broiler or toaster oven.

Edible Animals: Supply a variety of ingredients, and watch the children create ordinary and unusual creatures to gobble up. *Grrrr.*

Trains, Boats, and Planes: Graham crackers and a mixture of powdered sugar and milk are the ingredients for wood and cement, or brick and adobe. Have the children build whatever structure comes to mind, anything from a fort to a gingerbread house or a horse corral.

Don't stop now . . . Go on to the unexplored!

Materials: pretzels, cheese chunks; peanut butter, honey, powdered instant non-fat dry milk; English muffins, cheese slices, olives, tomato wedges, pizza sauce, anchovies, pepperoni; graham crackers, powdered sugar, milk

"Everything is art if it is chosen by the artist to be art."

Samuel Adams Green

Inventive Instruments 1:
Kid Creations

Have the children create their own instruments. Provide an assortment of noisemakers and containers. Have tape, glue, rubber bands, paper, and decorative materials ready. In a short time there will be homemade ukeleles, bongos, maracas, drums, guitars, and other instruments never before heard.

Play and sing songs together or accompany a favorite hit on the record player or radio.

Materials: beans, rice, pennies, popcorn, sand, cans, butter tubs, boxes, tape, clue, rubber bands, decorative materials

"After silence, that which comes nearest to expressing the inexpressible is music."

Aldous Huxley

Inventive Instruments 2:
K-K-Kazooooooo!

Cut a waxed paper circle large enough to overlap the end of a toilet paper tube one-half inch all around. Wrap the waxed paper tightly and put a rubber band around the rim of the tube to keep it on tight. Punch a hole in the tube near the papered end. Now hum into the open end. K-k-kazooooooo!!

Materials: waxed paper, scissors, toilet paper tubes, rubber bands

"When words leave off, music begins."

Heinrich Heine

Inventive Instruments 3:
Humming Quartet

Anyone can make a terrific sound and play a tune by using things on hand. Place a piece of paper across the back of a comb and hold the paper tightly on both sides. Hum into the comb. The vibration will create a note. Hum a tune to play a song. Experiment with different kinds of paper to get the perfect sound. Join together with other musicians and play favorite songs. Try "Michael Row the Boat Ashore." On someone's birthday, play "Happy Birthday to You!" During the holidays, play carols and fill the world with joy!

Materials: combs, paper

"Children are poor men's riches."

Thomas Fuller

Inventive Instruments 4:
Water Music

Make an instrument that has all eight notes of the musical scale. Simply line up eight water glasses on a table. Fill the first one with a small amount of water. Add more to the next and more to the third until you increase the water level to full by the eighth glass. Tap the glasses gently with a spoon or pencil. Vary the water levels slightly to get the notes of the scale correct. Then try a few simple songs, such as Old McDonald, Row, Row, Row Your Boat, Pop Goes the Weasel, or Jingle Bells.

Follow the numbers above the words to play Row, Row, Row Your Boat:

1 1 1 2 3
Row, row, row your boat,

3 2 3 4 5
Gently down the stream

8 8 8 5 5 5 3 3 3 1 1 1
Merrily, merrily, merrily, merrily,

5 4 3 2 1
Life is but a dream.

Which glass makes the highest note? Which one makes the lowest? Can you sing "do re mi fa so la ti do?" Try to put your favorite rhyme to music.

Materials: glasses, water, spoon or pencil

"So few have imagination that there are 10,000 fiddlers to one composer."

Charles F. Kettering

Mechanics at Work

The auto parts store must be open so the mechanics can get the parts they need. Inventory might include egg cartons, tin plates, plastic lids, empty boxes, aluminum foil, paper plates, etc.

Start with a large cardboard box as the body of the car. Let the children build any kind of vehicle they like — a police car, fire engine, taxi, bus, train, truck, etc. What parts should it have? The children may want to take a walk outside to look at a car. *A bumper? Yes! (Would an egg carton attached with brass brads work?) A steering wheel? Of course. (A paper plate can be attached with a brad in the middle so it will turn.) Headlights? Oh, yes. (Small tin plates or cupcake papers work well.) Wheels? (Use more paper plates.) What else?* (Beware, sometimes children want CB radios and ski racks. Be ready for creativity!) Let the children paint their vehicles at the end of the day. The next day they'll be ready for a trip, for work, or for who knows what! *Start 'em up and take off.*

Materials: cardboard boxes, paper plates, egg cartons, tape, brass brads, paint

"Invention is the mother of necessity."

Thorstein Veblen

82

Moving On

On another day, cut a hole in the bottom of each "vehicle" so that the children can stand up and move with their cars around their bodies. Set up road signs and teach the children to drive carefully. Show them how to wait for pedestrians, to stop at stop signs, and to obey a police officer directing traffic. Give each driver a real key.

Materials: road signs, police hat, whistle, roads of tape to follow, keys

"A school should not be a preparation for life. A school should be life."

Elbert Hubbard

Table-top Travelers

The children use various objects to create mountains, lakes, tunnels, fences, logs, and other such scenery in an imaginary countryside. Take miniature cars, animals, people, or imaginary characters on a journey over, under, around, and through the hazards, obstacles, and interesting sights as they become table-top travelers.

Materials: paper cups, plates, cardboard, utensils, pencils, boxes, cartons, fabric, etc.; masking tape to attach objects to table (optional)

"To bring up a child in the way he should go, travel that way yourself once in a while."

Josh Billings
(Henry Wheeler Shaw)

Water Wonder 1:
Air Powered Speedboat

Cut a half-gallon milk carton in half lengthwise and tape the end tightly closed. Make a small hole in the bottom end, and insert the tube of an inflated balloon. Vrrroooommmm! A motorboat! Put the boat in a small pool or the bathtub.

Motorboat, motorboat
Go so slow
Motorboat, motorboat
Go so fast
Motorboat, motorboat
Step on the gas!

Materials: milk cartons, scissor or knife, tape, balloons

"What is now proved was once only imagined."

William Blake

Water Wonder 2:
Nutty Sailboat

Use half of a walnut shell for the hull of a sailboat. Fill the inside with clay, and insert a toothpick for the mast. Cut a tiny sail out of paper, and poke the toothpick through at the top and bottom to hold it in place. Set out on the open seas (any body of water — a bucket, a pool, a bathtub, or even a lake formed in the sandbox). Since this boat is wind-powered, children will need to blow toward the sail to create a gentle breeze.

All mates will want to have a sailor's hat. Follow the directions below. Use an empty paper towel roll or just a hand to make a spyglass to look for land. Smooth sailing!

Materials: walnut shell halves, clay, toothpicks, paper

"We all live under the same sky, but we don't all have the same horizons."

Konrad Adenauer

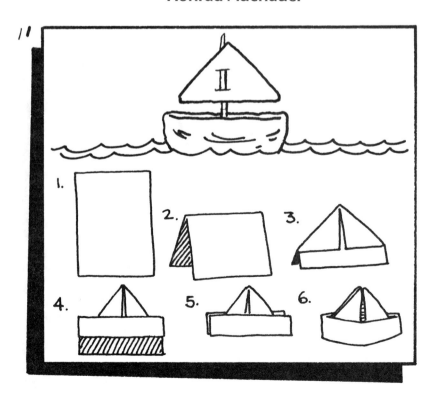

What Else???

Collect a few "common" items and set them aside. Choose one to begin. Hold it up, and then pass it around while everyone sings this chant:

Look, I have a <u>(wrench).</u>
Listen and touch and see.
Look, I have a <u>(wrench).</u>
What ELSE could this be?

"A robot's toothbrush!" (by Clint, age 4)
"A flower on Mars!" (by Paul, age 4)

*Possible items might be sandpaper, a spring, a wrench, a baby bottle, a flower vase, a lightbulb, tweezers. Any object is fun to try. Encourage divergent thinking. All answers are acceptable, of course.

Materials: common items

"Man's mind stretched by a new idea never goes back to its original dimensions."

Oliver Wendell Holmes

Wind Wonder 1:
Never-Fail Kites

Save plastic bread or produce bags. Each child will need one. Fold the top edge over about one inch. Poke a hole on each side and tie a piece of bright yarn through each hole. Add yarn on the bottom corners as "tails" if desired. That's all there is to it — the kite is complete.

*Even the youngest, most inexperienced child will be successful flying this kite. Simply run fast and hold the yarn up high!

Materials: plastic bags, yarn, scissors

"It is respectable to have no illusions — and safe, and profitable and dull."

Joseph Conrad

Wind Wonder 2:
Whirligig

Cut from each corner to the center of a five-inch square of paper, as shown. Bend alternate points to the center. Push a straight pin through all four points and the middle of the square into the eraser end of a pencil. (Use caution with sharp pins.) Take the whirligig outdoors, hold it high in the air, and run. It will whirl and spin around and around.

Materials: paper cut in 5" squares, pencils with eraser, straight pins

"One of the greatest sources of energy is pride in what you are doing."

unknown

Wind Wonder 3:
Flying Machines

Glider: Follow the folding diagram on the next page to make a glider. Then try adding weight to different parts of the glider with a lightweight paper clip or two and note the effect. Experiment with folding an extra flap on the wings to see how it changes the flight. Use different weights and textures of paper. Have a flying contest to see which plane will travel the farthest, which will glide the longest time in the air, and which has the smoothest landing.

Helicopter: Cut and fold paper according to the diagram on the next page. Hold the helicopter up as high as possible, then let it go. Watch it spin and whirl as it slowly descends. Experiment with this flying machine also. How can you change its flying time? How does weight affect the spinning speed?

Materials: paper, scissors, paper clips

> "Childhood is the world of miracle and wonder. The end of childhood is when things cease to astonish us. When the world seems familiar is when one has become an adult."
>
> Eugene Ionesco

Glider

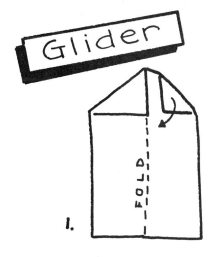

1.

FOLD

2.

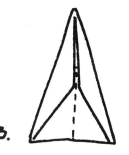

3.

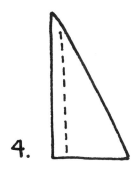

4.

5.

6.

Helicopter

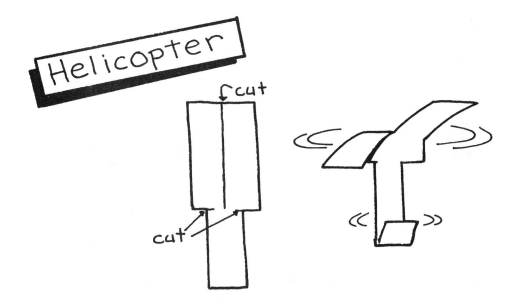

cut

cut

Sand Castle Construction

Put the children to work building a big and beautiful sand castle at the beach or in a sandbox with a bucket of water. Paper cups and cans make perfect molds for forming different-sized rooms or the protective wall around the royal castle. The children may choose to dig a moat and find something to use as a bridge, flag, or royal guardsman. It's a group effort of engineers, architects, sand sculptors, and decorators — a cooperative experience for all to enjoy.

*This kind of play provides invaluable fine motor and sensory experiences and helps children learn the concepts of weight, balance, porosity, and the interactions of different substances. These concepts aid in the children's eventual development of math and science skills.

Materials: sand, water, cups, cans, buckets, feathers, rocks, twigs, flowers, etc.

"Art is idea. It is not enough to draw, paint, and sculpt. An artist should be able to think."

Gordon Woods

PROJECTS

Adopt an Earthworm

Dig for worms after a rainy day. Fill a large jar mostly with soil and a small amount of sand. Put a layer of leaves on top and sprinkle with a few drops of water by hand. Put the earthworms in their newly decorated condominium. Cover the jar by wrapping it in black paper so it will be dark like an underground earthworm dwelling. Hang up an "occupied" sign. Serve a delicious dinner of small amounts of celery and lettuce pieces. Sprinkle on more water every few days. When the earthworms have had enough time to make themselves at home (several days), visit them by removing the paper and looking in.

*Since earthworms respond to vibrations, play instruments and watch them do a dance called the "Earthworm Wiggle." Have the children try it.

*Earthworms travel by stretch and squeeze movements. Have the children become earthworms by curling up tight, then walking out with hands and closing up with feet.

Materials: jar, soil, sand, leaves, water (do not overwater!), black paper, musical instruments (optional)

Adopt an Egg

Give each child a raw egg to "mother" or "father" for the day. Caring for the egg involves making a safe place for it when it is not being held, and finding a babysitter to take care of the egg while its "parent" is busy. Some children name their eggs and talk to them, rock them gently, sing songs to them, and even scold them. A sense of responsibility may grow between the child and the egg.

Materials: eggs

"Few things help an individual more than to place responsibility upon him, and to let him know that you trust him."

Booker T. Washington

All Together Now!

A real parachute is ideal for this activity, but a sheet with a hole cut in the middle to let air escape is the next best thing. Try these:

Everyone holds onto the edge of the parachute and lifts and lowers arms to create an ocean with swelling waves.

Try making a giant mushroom. Count to three — one, two, three — then everyone lifts the parachute high into the air and lets it slowly back down. On the count of three, up again! And again!

Next, sit down and make small waves while a few children walk on the water, then roll across the waves, and hop and jump on the waves.

Try having the children take turns lying down as the sheet is walked around them in a circle, first very slowly, then faster and faster and faster! Be sure to unwind by walking the other way also.

Now let one child stand in the middle as the sheet is wrapped around his body like a mummy. Then unwind.

Roll a child inside the sheet, then pull the end up and away and the child will roll free.

Place a small ball on the sheet and make a game of trying to keep the ball on the surface while everyone lets it roll close to the edge but not all the way off.

Play popcorn by putting many balls on the sheet and making them pop up and down. The fun is endless.

Materials: parachute or sheet, balls

"Imagination is the air of the mind."

P. J. Bailey

Barbershop

Decorate a Styrofoam cup with facial features. Paste or color eyes, eyebrows, a nose, and a mouth. How about a mustache? Rosy cheeks? Fill the cup about three-quarters full with dirt. Sprinkle the top with grass seed, then cover with dirt and pack lightly. Water every two or three days, and keep in a sunny place. When the grass grows, it becomes the person's hair. Give the children scissors, and set up a barbershop. Just a trim, please! Come back in a week for another!

Or make Potato People. Simply use a potato instead of a cup to plant the seeds. Scoop out one-half inch at the top, and plant as directed. Add facial features with a felt-tip marker. Put the potatoes in a cup or add toothpicks at the bottom for supports. Place near a window.

Materials: Styrofoam cups, colored paper or colored markers for facial features, dirt, grass seed, scissors; potatoes (optional)

"In bringing up children, spend on them half as much money and twice as much time."

Harold S. Hulbert

Beyond the City Limits

On a sunny day, take a box of colored chalk outdoors and let the children create a town or city with buildings, roads, intersections with traffic signs, railroads leading out of town past the factories and farms, lakes, streams, and other interesting roadside attractions — simply by drawing them to life on the sidewalk. Various "throwaway" items may be used to build bridges, tunnels, caves, waterfalls, and mountains. A rock may serve as a car, or a leaf may be an airplane. The children's imaginations will lead the way.

Materials: colored chalk, throw-away objects

"Life is short, but it's wide."

unknown

Break an Egg

Have a child close his eyes in anticipation of an egg being cracked open on his head. Break the pretend eggshell by tapping the child's head with the knuckles and making a "cluck" sound (with tongue rolled back in mouth). Then make the egg white and yolk run down the child's hair, over his cheeks, and onto his neck by running your fingers lightly over the child's head.

*This activity can make the senses come alive so that the "imaginary" feels just like the real thing. YUCK!

"No matter how unlikely a thing is, if it happens, it happens."

Stanislaw Lem

Bug Hotel

Cut out two sides of a half-gallon milk carton, and put the carton inside a nylon stocking. Tie a knot. This "hotel" makes a nice home for caterpillars, grasshoppers, beetles, and spiders. Dinner for the guests may include some leaves, grass, bits of bread, and **always** a capful of water. Check-out time is in one or two days. Guests get free transportation home, too!

Materials: half-gallon milk cartons, nylon stockings, scissors, bits of food, cap for water, bugs

"The true, strong and sound mind is the mind that can embrace equally great things and small."

Samuel Johnson

Cloudburst!

Cut out one side of several half-gallon milk cartons, and tape the ends tightly closed. Insert a straw through a hole at the bottom of each carton. Build several levels in a sandbox, and place a carton at each level. Pour water into the top carton, and it will empty through the straw into the next until it descends to the bottom. Watch for flash floods! Dig out a valley, and watch the water form a lake. Make small streams flow from the lake to "irrigate" farm lands.

*This is an activity that can be varied many ways. Try adding food coloring to one or more cartons to see what color you can create at the bottom. Or fill the top carton with ice, and sprinkle it with a watering can or garden hose. Help the children discover the effects of water flow by pointing out slides, erosion, and soil transportation.

Materials: half-gallon milk cartons, scissors or knife, tape, straws, sandbox, water; food coloring (optional)

"Action is the proper fruit of knowledge."

Thomas Fuller

A Gourmet Meal

Here are two ways of cooking up a feast fit for a fowl. First, make a bird-kabob by putting long pieces of string or yarn around or through pieces of fat cut from meat, peels of fruit, and whole peanuts. Hang the bird-kabob from a nearby tree.

For the main course, serve up a tasty treat by putting fat scraps in net bags that hang from the limbs of trees. Nail peels of fruit to the bark of the tree for fruit salad, and tie peanuts to twigs with bright pieces of yarn for a special surprise dessert. The birds will find the hidden treats inside the peanut shells.

Materials: string or yarn, net bags (such as those in which potatoes or onions are sold), peels of fruit, small nails or tacks, hammer, whole peanuts (in the shell)

"When a man has pity on all living creatures, then only is he noble."

Buddha

103

The Inside-Out Shirt

Draw the internal organs within the upper body on old tee shirts so that the children will be aware of the "machine" they have working at all times. Draw the lungs, heart, esophagus, intestines, and liver. Briefly tell the children what each part does for the body. Together, identify where someone would feel a stomach ache or the hiccups or "growling" or cramps. Where does food go? Where does air go? Listen to someone's chest. What noises does this "machine" make? How do we take care of our very special body machine?

Materials: old tee shirts, fabric markers

"There is so much to teach, and the time goes so fast."

Erma Bombeck

Moore Mud Sculptures

There's more to mud play than those delicious mud pies. Let the children work individually or in small groups to mush, pack, and build with gushy, yucky, messy mud to create beautiful art, like the famous sculptor Henry Moore.

Have the "artists" wear protective aprons so that they won't get mud or dirt on their clothing.

Materials: dirt, water, sculptor's tools (garden shovel, utensils, craft sticks, etc.), aprons

"Now I really make the little idea from clay, and I hold it in my hand. I can turn it, look at it from underneath, see it from one view, hold it against the sky, imagine it any size I like, and really be in control, almost like God creating something."

Henry Moore

Parachuters

To make parachutes, tie 12" strings to the corners of napkins or fabric squares. Gather the strings at the bottom, and tie them to a washer or other weighted object. Toss the parachute in the air, and watch it descend slowly, landing safely on the ground.

*This activity is a good example of air filling space, which creates the parachute effect.

Materials: square fabric, strings, scissors, washer

"If he is wise he does not bid you enter the house of wisdom, but rather leads you to the threshold of your own mind."

Kahlil Gibran

Pinecone Birdfeeder

Tie a piece of strong, bright yarn around the top of a pinecone. With fingers only, fill the spaces in the pinecone with peanut butter. Roll the sticky pinecone in wild bird seed, and it's ready to hang in a favorite tree. Be sure that the birds are able to perch on a nearby limb while eating from the feeder. Refill as needed.

Materials: pinecones, salt-free peanut butter, yarn, wild bird seed, paper plates (optional), foil to wrap the feeders to send home or give as gifts

"All nature is but art, unknown to thee."

Alexander Pope

Purely Amazing

Mazes are life-size puzzles for people. A true maze is made of bushes that form walls. Between them are narrow paths that lead in and out, and this way and that, and to many dead ends that lead no where at all. The trick is to find a way out.

Build a maze in miniature in the dirt, then try to drive a small car through it. Back up. Which path to choose? *Uh oh, dead end, try again.* Mazes on paper are fun, too. Ask someone else to make a maze, and then try to find the way out by drawing a path. Children can make mazes for their best friends. Be sure they use pencils to draw because it may take some changes to get it just right. Mazes usually have a center opening with many paths leading out. Try to make a maze with a center, and then draw many confusing paths from it. Be sure to have turns and bends and lots of dead ends. Don't forget the exit route. Try it to be sure there is a way to escape successfully. How would it be to explore a real life-size maze?

Materials: paper, pens, pencils with erasers; toy cars or people (optional)

"You will never amount to much."

Munich schoolmaster to Albert Einstein

108

Sunbelt Snowmen

Living in a warm climate doesn't have to mean missing the opportunity to build snowmen. Consider these creative alternatives!

Thorny the Tumbleweed Man: Stack tumbleweeds for the body and head. Poke leaves into the neck area for the scarf. The traditional carrot nose and charcoal eyes may be used, or better yet, search around and find something even more suitable.

Sifty the Sandman: Build him lying flat on the beach. Mound sand to form his body and head. Wrap seaweed to make his scarf, and add shells and feathers for his eyes and nose? What would make a good hat?

Leo the Leafman: He, too, can be flat on the grass. Gather leaves to form his body and head. Use a few large leaves to make a hat, or a real one will do. How about seed pods for his eyes? Acorns? Pinecones for his nose?

Materials: hat and scarf (optional); local natural treasures

"The greatest mistake of all is to do nothing."

Charles Kettering

Up, Up, and Away!

Each child may think of a secret message to send, or together the group may want to think of messages. Sometimes it's fun to draw a self-portrait and include some information about yourself with a request that you be contacted if the message is found. Roll up the message paper and insert it in a latex balloon. Go to a nearby florist or balloon shop and have the balloons filled with helium. Then . . . separately or all at the same time . . . let them go. Up, up, and away. Keep an eye on your balloon until it is completely out of sight. It may be days, weeks, or months, but some day you may hear from someone who has found your message. Where do they live? How far away did your balloon travel?

Materials: latex balloons, paper, pen, helium

"I like the dreams of the future better than the history of the past."

Thomas Jefferson

What I Want To Be

Have each child lie on a large piece of butcher paper and outline the body. When complete, have the children dress themselves in appropriate attire for what they want to be when they grow up. A firefighter? They will need a red suit, heavy black boots, and a firefighter's hat. A mommy? They might have a baby in their arms or at their side and wear pretty earrings and carry a purse. A doctor? They might have a white coat and wear a stethoscope. Cut out the life-size pictures and mount them for display.

Materials: large white butcher paper, tracing crayon, crayons or paints, scissors

"My mother had a great deal of trouble with me, but I think she enjoyed it."

Mark Twain

Rain Check

On those occasions when there isn't time to tell that special story, give that lesson in bike-riding, or that chance to visit a friend, give a "rain check" for later. The children will know that the special time will come again soon.

*Children often want immediate attention. Rain checks may help them understand that occasionally a special time must be delayed.

Materials: paper, pen

"Life is a series of experiences, each one of which makes us bigger, even though sometimes it is hard to realize this."

Henry Ford